BREWING BETTER BEERS

by Ken Shales

A PRACTICAL GUIDE TO THE CRAFT
WHICH WILL SATISFY EVERY WOULD-BE
HOME BREWER — AND HIS THIRST!

Amateur Winemaker Publications

Published by
Argus Books Limited
1 Golden Square
London W1R 3AB
England

© Argus Books Limited 1984

2nd Edition 1981
4th Impression 1985

ISBN 0 900841 64 8

Printed in Great Britain by
Standard Press (Andover) Ltd., South Street, Andover, Hants.
Telephone: Andover 59411

BREWING BETTER BEERS

THIS book is dedicated to the Rt. Hon. Reginald Maudling, Esq., M.P., who in his Budget of 1963 legalised the brewing of beer at home without licence or restriction, thereby righting a wrong of over eighty years standing.

K.S.

FOREWORD

Beer is one of the oldest alcoholic drinks known to mankind. In adding yet another work to the catalogue I have had a lot of fun, and made a lot of beer and many helpful friends.

There are not a great many recipes in this book, for it is my belief that the mere compilation of recipes is not likely to advance the Craft very much. Instead I have tried to put across, insofar as my capabilities permit, the reasoning behind the recipe. Nobody can claim mastery of the Craft until he or she is able to formulate any desired beer and produce it, starting from a clean sheet of paper.

KEN SHALES
Basildon, 1967

FOREWORD to the 2nd Edition

The 1st Edition of Brewing Better Beers was published in 1967 and since then the book has sold some 308,965 copies. Eighteen impressions have been printed since the author's death, in 1971, and the publishers have regularly revised, up-dated and re-illustrated this popular handbook.

THE BALLAD OF BOOZELDON

by Ken Shales

I am a happy booze runner, with a production line,
I've set the town of Boozledon awash with beer and wine.
For years I have been brewing, it always was tax free,
Though it wasn't really legal 'till the year of '63.

We brew it by the dustbin, and drink it by the pail.
You name it and we'll make it, lager, stout or ale.
If our stocks are running low, somebody will shout,
"Let's have a drop of heavy in, and lay these fellows out."

We are all good noshers too, just every kind of dish,
Steak and chips, or Goulash, or even Flying Fish.
Pies of Cheese and Bacon or a bowl of Cook-up Rice.
Roll mops and Heimishers, all are very nice.

A cheerful band of drinkers, together we all stand,
Maybe a bit unsteady, with tankards in the hand.
Prentices or Craft Brothers, we have our little joke,
We are always drinking, but the Publicans go broke!

CONTENTS

BREWING GLOSSARY

ACETIC ACID:
The acid of vinegar, should not be present in sound beer.

ALE:
A top fermenting beer, as opposed to lager. Formerly used to signify an unhopped beverage.

BEER:
General term to signify a fermented beverage made from malted barley or other grains, usually hopped.

CONDITION:
The amount of carbon dioxide dissolved in the beer. Some lagers can carry as much as 7 grams per litre.

CYTASE:
An enzyme which removes the cellulosic coating of starch granules.

DIASTASE:
A starch-breaking enzyme (see Mashing).

ENZYME:
A complex protein molecule capable of acting as a catalyst in biochemical reactions.

FININGS:
A gelatinous substance used to precipitate suspended matter in beer.

FOB:
Froth.

HOP:
A flower used to impart bitterness and keeping properties to beer.

HOP PELLETS:
Shredded and reconstituted hop cones.

IRISH MOSS:
Dried sprigs of special seaweed used as finings.

ISINGLASS:
See Finings.

KRAUSEN:
To cause condition to develop in a beer by adding a percentage of fermenting wort.

LAGER:
A bottom fermented beer.

LAMBIC:
A rare Belgian beer, unique in that it is fermented by a wild yeast. Not to everybody's taste.

MALT:
Grain, usually barley which has been germinated and dried. Available in various grades.

MASHING:
The reaction between the enzyme diastase and starch which produces fermentable sugars.

NATURALLY CONDITIONED:
Beer in which the CO_2 has been formed *in situ* by yeast, as opposed to carbonated beer where it is forced in by pressure. Naturally conditioned beers have better flavour but are disadvantageous commercially.

PITCH:
To inoculate a wort with yeast.

QUASSIA:
A bitter wood, formerly used to adulterate beer by replacing hops.

RACK:
To siphon clear beer from a deposit.

ROUSE:
To stir vigorously from the bottom of vessel.

SPARGE:
To wash by sprinkling with water. Derived from the same root as asparagus, bunches of which were used by ancient Greek priests to sprinkle holy water.

STERILISATION:
Destruction of bacteria by heat or chemicals.

STOUT:
A black beer of high gravity, usually bitter.

SIPHON:
See Rack.

WORT:
Unfermented beer—analogous to "must" in wine-making.

CHAPTER I

EQUIPPING A HOME BREWERY

"He who would have much to do, let him try fitting out a ship – or a woman" – old Proverb

Fortunately a home brewery does not fit into either of those categories. In fact, my own outfit, which can produce 250 gallons a year with ease, and could do even more in an emergency, cost far less than many people will pay for an electric drill.

It *is* possible to go berserk and spend very large sums of money, but I do not advise it. Start in a small way, with household equipment, and progress to more elaborate things later, when once you have the hang of it.

A point which I never tire of repeating is that it pays handsomely to join the local wine circle. Somebody there is sure to know the dealers in jars and such items in the vicinity. You will also have a chance to see somebody's brewery in operation, and learn all sorts of things which are not in books.

In olden times, houses often had a washhouse cum scullery outside of the main building. This, and a cellar, would enable you to produce amounts far beyond the normal usage of a household, even if parties were held twice a week and beer was drunk at every meal. Steak and a pint of Double Daphne is quite a fair breakfast, by the way. Not being favoured with extensive premises, I have to use the cupboard under the stairs and occasional use of the kitchen. Avoid the "ventilated larders" for the fermentation or maturing of beer. They are too cold in winter. Whatever place you use, it will pay to put plenty of shelves in it. Those for the gallon or two gallon jars to rest on must be well made and Rawlplugged into the wall. Lighter shelves at the top are ideal for storage of packets of malt, hops, etc. It is helpful to have a heater and thermostat in the fermenting cupboard, but not essential, as long as the house is not left unheated for days at a time in winter. Even then, it is only beer in the first fermentation which will be affected. The thermostated heater will, however, enable you to time your fermentations almost to the hour. Nevertheless, it is something that I haven't installed yet, but my family are always good at closing doors and keeping large fires in, which may explain this. It may pay to have a lock on the fermentation cupboard if you have toddlers or inquisitive cats on the premises. I actually heard of a cat getting a beer shampoo, in a 4 gallon brew of stout. Neither was improved by it!

A supply of hot water is not essential, but very helpful, one of those gas heaters which can deliver water at anything up to the boiling point being particularly recommended. You wouldn't install one just for brewing, but it may well be the decisive factor in your case.

Now for the plant. Beer worts must be well boiled, and since the general batch size for home brewers is about four gallons, it is necessary to use a pot with a working capacity of two gallons. I use a "waterless cooker" that we were talked into buying years ago, in our green and salad days. Somehow the food never did taste right, but the consensus of opinion is that the beer is excellent. For small scale trials a large saucepan could be used. An ex-army dixie, or a large fish kettle, could be used and the small galvanised wash boilers to put on a gas stove are handy and not dear. Small gas or electric wash boilers may be used. So long as no acids are used, the metal of which it is made is not important, lead excepted. Stainless steel is the easiest to keep clean but very dear.

For boiling water: saucepan or Burco boiler.

10

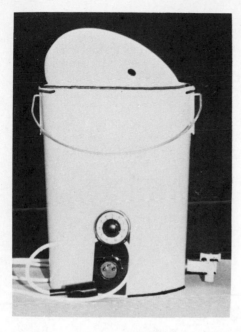

If you are going to brew regularly, it is well worth buying Ritchie's Bruheat boiler.

It is thermostatically controlled, and ideal for boiling, mashing, and even fermenting.

For a first fermentation vessel half casks or large "Ali Baba" stoneware jars can be used, or the traditional "bread pan" if one can be found. Quite frankly, however, all these are obsolete, and I would recommend the purchase of a polythene fermentation bin with lid. Calibrate it in gallons, and an extra mark at four gallons two or three pints. They are translucent enough to see the liquid level outside, so just cut little nicks in the ribs at each point, and put a drop of black undercoat in it. Plastic buckets are useful for small brews, and also for draining washed beer bottles, eight to ten being put upside down in each. Some types of photographic chemicals now come in 15-litre calibrated buckets. These are retangular in shape and have a fitting lid. For your second stage fermentation I have not yet found anything to beat the one gallon or two gallon jar, fitted with corks and fermentation locks. Glass is best, since one can see that settling has proceeded properly before bottling. For the final stage of the beer one has the choice of draught or bottled. Casks are not much good for the amateur, since they are hard to keep clean and sweet, and maintenance is very difficult. Moreover, they don't hold the head very long.

There are now a host of pressure barrels and CO_2 injector systems on the market, satisfying the home brewers' desire for draught beer.

Conventional Style Barrel

Plastic barrels, mainly in the conventional style, have been completely redesigned and are now a substantial product. Most are fitted with a threaded tap insert of acetal plastic which is sturdier than the barrel itself. One small snag is that the insert does not like continual contact with sterilising liquids so do not leave such solution in the barrel when it is empty.

Barrel sizes vary between 10-50 litres, some with a wood grain effect of staves, others are translucent, thus showing the beer level at a glance. Some have carrying handles, others indentations forming lifting devices.

The large majority have a filler cap designed to take a CO_2 gas injector system.

For the bottled beer, one can use pint or quart screw stoppered beer bottles, for which spare washers should be kept, or cider bottles, though these are sometimes 26ozs which is an odd size if you use pint tankards. If neither of these types of bottles are available in your area the crown corked type of bottle may be used. Retailers supply plastic caps, which really do hold the pressure, at a small price, or one can buy a crown corking machine and caps.

A typical crown corker in operation.

For straining purposes one needs a colander, preferably plastic, or some other means of supporting a piece of muslin for straining the wort. Terylene curtain net is a much better proposition than cotton, it lasts for years, and does not get stained. After all, Terylene was used as an industrial filter cloth years before the housewife ever heard of it. Six feet of $\frac{1}{4}$ inch i.d. plastic tubing is needed for siphoning, a couple of inches of soft rubber tube can be fitted to one end to help bottling. A small plastic tap is easily fitted, and a little plastic "rose" to the other will avoid stirring up sediments. Funnels are best made of polythene. Stirring paddles should be made from some non-resinous wood. A quart jug marked in fluid ounces is very nearly essential. Kitchen scales are helpful, but can be dispensed with.

Having equipped the brewery, it is essential to see that everything is clean before use. The methods here apply to normal practice as well as when commissioning a new brewery.

CHAPTER II

CLEANLINESS

Beers and beer worts are almost ideal media for growing a large variety of bacteria, yeasts and moulds. Even dry rot (Merulius Lachrymans) can be grown on malt preparations. In the average kitchen spores of many different yeasts can be found, from fruits and baking of bread. If winemaking is carried on, wine yeasts will be present, and must be kept out of beer.

The ordinary rules of hygiene must be observed, but for our purpose, more drastic means of sterilisation have to be resorted to. Sterilising agents must not possess strong odours, or be toxic to the growth of the appropriate yeast. Pine fluid and the like are definitely out.

The most popular sterilising agent used is sulphur dioxide. Formerly it was produced by burning brimstone, a method which is still used occasionally.

Siphons of the liquified gas can be purchased, but are not practical for our purpose. Commercial brewers use the bi-sulphite of lime, but the home brewer uses sodium meta-bisulphite, or Campden tablets, which are the potassium salt. The most simple way of using bisulphite is to make up a 10% solution, i.e. 2oz in a pint, and dispense it from a squeeze bottle. Old washing-up liquid bottles are readily available, and free!

When putting away jars, fermentation bins and the like, a few drops will keep them clean and sweet. For routine sterilisation of apparatus, 1fl oz of your stock solution made up to 6oz and a level teaspoonful of citric acid is used. The bottles are rinsed free of yeast, then swilled round with the solution, which is poured back in the jug. Care must be taken to ensure that every part of the bottles comes into contact with the solution. The bottles are rinsed twice with tap water and drained. Sterile bottles, stoppered, can be put aside for the next brew. The same 6oz will be adequate for at least 40 bottles, but it must be discarded afterwards.

It is false economy to try to save it, because the loss of a whole brew could result. It has happened, but not to me! Yeast will tolerate a little sulphur dioxide, and in fact that is the sole preservative allowed in beer in the UK.

Bottles can be sterilised by heat, but this is not very practical at home, on the scale of brewing operations.

There is a good range of sterilising agents on the market – Chempro, Silana, VWP for instance, which have devolved from the commercial brewery, which clean, sterilise and deodorise in one operation. The ordinary household bleaches diluted to 10% are suitable. Neat bleach will destroy organic deposits.

When one is bringing second-hand containers into use for the first time, use a stronger solution of your sterilizer together with a good bottle brush. A 10 minute soak and a good scrub, will soon restore that pristine sparkle. If a brush can't be got into the bottle, a fathom of brass lamp chain swirled round is most efficacious. Get a length from Woolworths and keep it handy. It is one of the most useful tools in a home-brewer's kit. Some use small stones for this purpose. Lead shot is not advisable, because particles of lead can adhere to the bottle, and cause poisonous beer. So far as I know there are no Borgias in wine circles nowadays although some brews one meets cause one to think a bit hard at times.

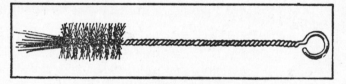

A handy bottle brush.

Washing bottles is rather a tedious business, which consumes much time and is rather unpopular with everybody. It seems never to come to an end, and shaking is rough on the arm muscles.

THE EQUIPMENT TO GET
YOU GOING

Large saucepan or boiling pan, plastic
fermentation bin with lid, 2m length of plastic
tubing used for siphoning the beer into bottles
or barrel, nylon sieve, ex wine 5 cube, 1 gallon
demijohn, thermometer, airlock, funnel, beer
bottles, crown caps and corker.

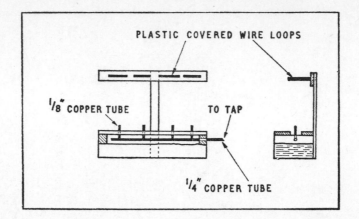

PLASTIC COVERED WIRE LOOPS

$\frac{1}{8}$" COPPER TUBE

TO TAP

$\frac{1}{4}$" COPPER TUBE

The "Ken Shales Rinsemaster" has changed that! This is a simple apparatus which cuts down the shaking and deals with four bottles at once. The prototype is a bit of very rough carpentry, mainly because I am not much of a chippy and, anyway, my workshop is piled up with spare brewing gear!

The basis of the apparatus is a length of copper tubing, about $\frac{1}{4}$in. bore, with one end sealed, and the other, by means of a length of hose and a standard fitting, connected to the tap.

At intervals 3in lengths of $\frac{1}{8}$in copper tube are affixed, by drilling and soldering. It will be found that not all these jets deliver the same amount of water, and the simplest way of adjusting this is to apply solder to the ends, and ream out until the jets throw to the same height.

This spray unit is fixed to a fairly substantial block of wood. Two small cross pieces are nailed on, and two strips of wood lengthwise, for the necks of the bottles to rest upon and allow the water to run out.

A support for the bottles is provided by a wooden T piece with loops made of plastic covered wire. Simple, isn't it? Drop your bottles on, apply 10 seconds spray, turn off and put them upside down to drain in a plastic bucket. Unless the family has a well developed sense of humour though, remember to put a bottle over *all* the jets! The drawing should make it all clear, but if it doesn't, please remember that I only have a "ticket" for ASTMS, not DATA!

This gadget should save hours in a year; maybe somebody will make it commercially in plastic covered wire or the like. In which case I want my royalties in some non-taxable form, like sugar or grape juice!

CHAPTER III

BEER KITS

Kit beers are estimated to hold 80% of the Homebrewing market, with the 40 pint kit well to the fore. The main advantage is the speed and ease of getting the brew fermenting. The average time spent from entering the kitchen, to completing the brew, washing up and retiring to your chair is about 20 minutes. The longest time spent is waiting for 4 pints of water to boil.

The growth of Lager sales is one of the features in the boom of the market, taking up some 50% of the kits sold. A vast number of dry or wet kits, ranging from 8-40 pints, are available from your specialist shop, chemists or stores.

Instructions on making the brew obviously vary slightly, but basically you boil 4 pints of water, take it off the heat, dissolve around 1kg or 2lbs sugar in the water, pour in your can of malt extract, stir well and then tip it into your fermentation bucket. Top up with cold water to the amount you are making. Check that the temperature of the wort is between 18-23°C (65-75°F), sprinkle in your yeast and cover. After about five days the S.G. will have fallen to 1006 and the fermentation stopped.

Siphon off into your keg or bottles, priming them at the rate of $\frac{1}{2}$ teaspoon of sugar per pint or 2oz to the barrel. Keep in a warm atmosphere for around seven days so that the secondary fermentation gets underway, and then move to a cool spot 10-13°C (50-55°F) for storage. Normally your beer is ready for drinking in three weeks. It will improve with age and I have heard of it being kept for up to 18 months without deterioration, but somehow I never get beyond the three month stage.

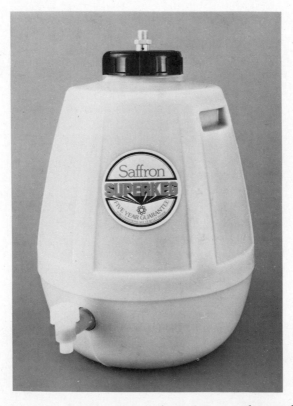

One of the many pressure kegs now on the market.

CHAPTER IV

Ingredients:– Malt and Grains

The base of all recognisable beers is Malt.

Barley grain contains the embryo plant and its food reserve in the form of starch, which is insoluble in cold water. When the barley is malted, it is first steeped in water and allowed to sprout until the tip of the seedling just reaches the other end of the husk. During this time an enzyme, cystase, dissolves the cellulose covering each starch granule, and a further enzyme, diastase, is produced, which is capable of splitting up starch into a mixture of simple sugars. These are water soluble and can be fermented by yeast to produce alcohol and carbon dioxide. In a brewery this splitting up of starch is carried out in hot water between 63-68°C (145° and 155°F) for a number of hours. This process is called "mashing". The full mashing process is messy and time consuming. It is generally dispensed with by home brewers in favour of Malt Extract. Malt Extract can be purchased as a syrup, containing 20% water, or as a dry powder. It is more economical to buy 14lb or 28lb at a time from specialist manufacturers or suppliers. Malt extracts are made for many other purposes besides brewing, and incorrect grades, such as for bakery purposes, cannot be made to yield good beer. The kind for children, containing cod liver oil, is definitely useless for our purpose. In addition to malt extract, other kinds of grain products are of great use in home brewing. A good grade of home brewing malt extract, such as Edme Ltd's DMS, contains enough diastase to convert about 20% of its weight of added starch, if the process is carried out correctly. Some grades of grain malt do not need "mashing" but may be simply boiled to extract their contents. The principal types available are crystal malt and patent black malt.

CRYSTAL MALT

If you take a grain of crystal malt and cut it, you will see that it is dark coloured, like toffee, inside. Unlike pale malt it does not need mashing to get a good extract, because it is treated in such a way that the saccharification is carried out in the drying kiln. This is why it is included in so many of the home brew packets.

The use of crystal malt in home brew gives increased colour, good body, and a full roundness on the palate. It is not desirable to use solely this quality of malt, since it would lead to cloying, heavy taste, and possibly difficulty in fermenting out the last few degrees, since not all sugars are as readily fermentable as others. According to the kind of beer required, the rest of the wort can be made from other types of malt, malt extract, and sugar.

My household beer is made on a basis of crystal malt, D.M.S. malt extract and white sugar. I don't know what to class it as, since it is not a light ale, nor is it really a pale ale, it is not a bitter, and it is not strong enough to be a barley wine! So my small daughter gets the honour, and it is called Double Daphne.

DOUBLE DAPHNE

(recipe for 4 gallons)
Ingredients:

335g	($\frac{3}{4}$lb)	Crystal malt
900g	(2lb)	D.M.S.
55g	(2oz)	Hops
113kg	(3lb)	Sugar
		1 level teaspoonful plaster of Paris

6.75litre (1$\frac{1}{2}$gallons) Water
Original gravity 1.052

Method:

Crack the malt grains, bring all the ingredients to the boil and hold for 30 minutes. Strain on to 1.3kg (3lb) of granulated sugar and make up to just over 18 litres (4 gallons), using part of the water to wash the spent grains. Cool to 25°C and pitch with a good ale yeast (I use Red Label Bass strain, but excellent varieties can be bought). After 24 hours or so, skim. If one uses a fermentation bucket and lid the skimming is often done automatically, the yeast adhering to the lid and sides, which is then washed off. After seven days siphon off into one- or two-gallon jars with fermentation locks. Leave a week, then bottle into pint beer bottles, adding half teaspoonful of white sugar to each. Leave at least 10 days, three weeks if possible. If the work has been carried out properly there will be a very slight sediment, no more than a paint coat, at the bottom of each bottle.

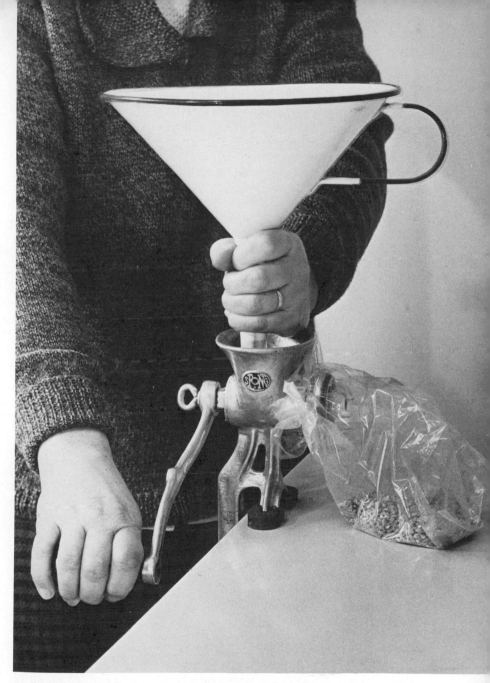

One of the basic ways of cracking malt. Malt must be cracked before
being mashed.

PATENT BLACK MALT

This is another specialised type of malt grain, made by roasting malt to the point at which fumes are evolved. This results in the almost complete destruction of the enzymes, and a drastic alteration of the carbohydrate components of the grain. The resulting product has a very low extract, i.e. it adds very little strength to the wort, but adds a very distinctive colour and flavour to the beer, a sort of astringent, woody effect, which is characteristic of stout. Small additions of this malt can be used to colour beers, but if one makes a range, it could lead to them all having a similar flavour; which is pointless.

Stouts are all high gravity dark beers, varying from a fulsome sweetness to a distinctive sharp bitterness. Stout is a typical product of British (or should I say Irish?) brewing techniques, and owes nothing to Continental inspiration. The so-called "milk stouts", a name now outlawed under the Labelling of Food Orders, were made by the addition of lactose (sugar of milk). This is not fermentable by brewers yeast, and so remains behind in the finished beer. Lactose can be bought from home-brew suppliers at reasonable cost.

It should be fully soluble in water, and have no odour or taste other than sweetness.

This recipe gives a good dark stout, about the middle of the range, which can be sweetened by the addition of lactose at the rate of 110g (4ozs.) per gallon, added in solution at racking.

BASILDON STOUT

(recipe for 4 gallons)
Ingredients:

225g	(8oz.)	Patent black malt
900g	(2lb.)	malt extract
55g	(2oz.)	hops
		1 teaspoon salt

6.75 Litre (1½ gallons) water
Original gravity 1.052

Method:
Bring to the boil, simmer for half an hour, strain on to 1.3kg (3lb) of coarse sugar (the darkest available) wash spent grains, make up to just over 4 gallons. Cool to not above 28°C. and pitch with a suitable yeast, either a culture derived from Guinness bottles or such as Leigh-

Williams Vinotex stout yeast. The appropriate yeast seems to make a lot of difference in the flavour of this class of beer.

Allow to ferment for five to seven days. Rack into 1 or 2 gallon jars, fit locks and leave for another week. Bottle in pint bottles, adding $\frac{1}{2}$ teaspoon of white sugar to each, leave two or three weeks to develop condition. It is very rare to experience settling troubles in this type of beer, probably because the black malt has substances precipitant in their effect.

FLAKED BARLEY

This is obtainable from corn chandlers and home brewing specialists. It is clean and easy to mash, provided that excessive amounts are not used. It gives body and a crisp grainy taste to a beer, and is especially useful in Pale Ale and Irish Stout types of beer.

FLAKED MAIZE

This is very useful in light and mild ales, and to some extent in lagers. It should not be overdone. It is well to note that one of the reasons why American beers do not suit the European palate is because of the large amounts of "corn" and corn products used in their making.

WHEAT

Wheat has been used for a long while, both raw and malted. It was used in Elizabethan England to make specially strong ales, and such products as Berliner Weissbier were all wheat. It is apparently still used in various special local brews in Belgium. The main reason for the small usage of malted wheat seems to be that it is difficult to malt, as the young shoot immediately comes out of the grain, and is liable to be damaged in "turning the piece". Barley shoots do not emerge for some days, and in fact "overshot" malts are liable to be rejected for brewing.

It is possible to malt wheat at home, but it is a tedious business, and unless one gets a good sample of seed grain, germination is not level. From the taste of it I guess that wheat malt should make a fair mild ale, but unless a few pounds come my way, this must remain a guess.

RICE

Rice, whole or flaked, can be used, but the trials I have made were not encouraging, the whole rice gave a poor extract, the flakes a better one, but prolonged mashing times seemed to be necessary, there was difficulty in getting clarity, and the resulting beer seemed to produce a headache the next day, out of proportion to the pintage consumed. Paddy rice I have not tried, malted rice I have heard of but never seen. Sake is not, according to my information, made by malting and mashing to produce a wort beer-wise, but by using the "Koji ferment" to deal with a thick starchy rice gruel. This ferment is supposed to be a symbiont of several moulds and yeasts, and to produce high concentrations of alcohol in very short periods. Could be useful, to say the least, if only to make high alcohol neutral wines for blending.

OATS

Small amounts of oat malt are reputed to be made, but I have never met any. Porridge oats are not very much use in home brew, as they seem to take ages to mash, and yield no advantage in flavour. Since the Labelling of Food Order was imposed very few stouts are now labelled "Oatmeal" in any case.

RYE

I have seen recipes for stout using rye, but until recently could not find any to experiment with.

I made up one of my most popular stouts, "Finn MacCool", using rye to replace the flaked barley. My tasting panel all noticed the difference, but gave it the same degree of acceptance. It seems to be smoother and have a slightly greater head retention. Further lines of research will no doubt suggest themselves to a keen brewer.

RYE-FINN

Prior to brewing the rye grain was coarsely milled in an electric coffee grinder and soaked overnight.

Ingredients:

450g	(1lb)	patent black malt (coffee milled)
900g	(2lb)	sugar
85g	(3oz)	hops
225g	(8oz)	crystal malt (coffee milled)
450g	(1lb)	rye
900g	(2lb)	malt extract
		mild ale water treatment (L.W.), *q.v.* to suit water

6.75 litres (1½ gallons) water

Method:

Mash at 65°C (150°F) for three-quarters of an hour, bring to the boil, add hops (3oz). Boil for half an hour, strain on to white sugar (2lb). Sparge hops, make the wort up to $4\frac{1}{4}$ gallons, cool to 21°C (70 °F), and pitch with a brewer's yeast ("R.L.B. strain"). Ferment five to seven days, rack into jars under locks, leave for five to seven days, bottle in 1 pint bottles with half a teaspoonful of white sugar to each one. Mature for three weeks before drinking.

BREWING FLOUR

This is a specialised wheat flour of graded particle size, used by commercial breweries and now available to the amateur. I tried it in standard brews as a replacement for flaked maize and flaked barley.

The first thing noticed was that the brewing flour was very much more readily attacked by the diastase in the malt extract than the maize. The wort came out brighter than usual, and presumably due to this product being totally convertible, the O.G. of the brew was slightly higher.

Fermentation proceeded at the normal rates, but it was noted that in the second stage the beers tended to clear fractionally faster than usual. The finished beers were noticeably smoother in palate, but the taste remained clean, and were regarded as an improvement by all the tasting panel. Head retention seemed a little better than usual.

In general it was concluded that the product was definitely worthwhile, giving real improvements in several directions, which more than justified the slight increase in cost. The properties of brewing flour suggest that it would be useful in the formulation of sweet stouts.

The intelligent use of malt adjuncts marks the skilled home brewer, and I certainly am glad to have brewing flour as an addition to my armoury.

CHAPTER V

SUGAR

It is impossible to make a fermented beverage without the use of sugar in some form or other. For many centuries, however, the sugar content was derived either from fruit, honey or the splitting of starches by malting and mashing grains. The cheap, readily available and extremely pure supplies of cane sugar are in fact a feature of modern technology and enterprise. Beet sugar is chemically identical, and is not distinguishable in our craft.

There is no point in using any other grade of white sugar than the ordinary granulated variety. **"Candy sugar"** is a hang-over from the primitive days of the industry, when a pure product was made by very slow crystallisation. You can get it, but it is a waste of money. **Treacle** and **Golden Syrup** can be used in brewing, but quite honestly, I cannot recommend either.

The taste is characteristic and persistent, and just does not give a clean palate to the beer. You *may* like it in some stouts, but even the best golden syrup will ruin any pretensions to quality in a pale or bitter beer.

So, if you simply wish to raise the alcoholic strength of a beer, without altering the colour or flavour, up to 60% of your fermentable carbohydrates can consist of white sugar. It is not good practice to exceed this, even in very heavy beers, because the beer will then drink very thin for its gravity. For very light beers, and lagers, much less sugar should be used, even down to none at all.

Barbados, "Soft Brown" or "Foot Sugar" are helpful in the making of brown ales and some stouts, where the raw sugar flavour carries over into the finished beer, and is a much-liked feature of the type.

The very pale Demerara does not impart very much flavour or colour, and just adds to the cost, without necessity. Save it for your coffee!

In general, get the darkest kind available, and blend it with a proportion of ordinary white sugar according to your requirements. When using samples of raw sugar, remember that it is possible for them to contain wild yeasts and ferments adverse to the beer, so that it is wise to ensure sterility by boiling.

29

Invert Sugar is often use in home-brewing, and is prepared mainly by acid treatment of cane sugar, either at home, or industrially. For a comparison of their properties refer to the chapter "Designing and Experimenting". These products are, of course, marginally faster in fermentation than the non-inverted sugars, but the yeast carries enzymes capable of handling the job in due course.

Commercial breweries also use a type of invert sugar derived from the acid hydrolysis of starches (grain or potato for example). These are usually delivered as a syrup, in bulk, and are not likely to be available to the amateur user at a competitive price. The main reason for the cheapness of granulated white sugar is that everybody uses it, and it is handled efficiently and in bulk, everywhere in the country. The amount of invert sugars used by home brewers is hardly likely to make it worth anybody's while to handle these sticky syrups in small amounts.

"Black invert", prepared by the inversion of specially selected grades of unrefined sugar, is definitely worthwhile for the amateur brewer. This is found in a syrup form, about 80% solids, and is used to impart the characteristic flavour and colour to "brown ales". For myself, I was weaned on IPA and rarely drink a commercial brown ale, but they are exceedingly popular, especially in the South. In hot weather they are very easy to drink!

Some sugars owe their place in the brewer's armoury to the fact that they are not fermentable by yeast. The principal example is **lactose,** the sugar of milk, which is used to make the sweet, fulsome type of stout formerly called "Milk Stout". Additions of up to two ounces per gallon are sufficient. It can be had from chemists, but is often rather expensive. Semplex stock it, at a reasonable price, and if you enjoy this type of beer it is worth a try.

The sugars in crystal malt, due to its special process of manufacture, are not all readily fermentable. This makes it especially suitable for rounding off a beer, as in the formulation of milds, browns, and heavy, keeping beers of the "Yuletide" type.

As an example of the use of black invert sugar here is a brown ale based on it. The sugar in question was obtained from Manbré Sugars Ltd, who do not normally deal in small amounts, but perhaps some of the home-brew suppliers may be interested in retailing it.

KEN'S BROWN ALE

Ingredients:

225g	(8oz)	crystal malt
225g	(8oz)	flaked maize
675g	(1½lb)	malt extract
785g	(1¾lb)	black invert sugar
55g	(2oz)	hops
		Water treatment, as for mild ales, eg salt or a proprietary article such as LW Mild Ale Crystals
		Caramel, *q.s.* (about 3 teaspoons)

6.7 litres (1½ gallons) water

Method:

Mash at 65°C (150°F) or as close as possible for 30 minutes, bring to the boil, add hops (2oz); boil for 30 minutes, strain on to Black invert sugar (1¾lb), make up to 4¼ gallons. Pitch with a brewer's yeast when not over 27°C (80°F), ferment for about five days, rack into gallon jars with locks, bottle after one week into pint bottles, priming with ½ teaspoon white sugar to each. Mature for two to three weeks. Heading liquid may be added to the first fermentation after three or four days.

CARAMEL

Caramel colouring can be purchased from your specialist shop or chemists (or as liquid gravy browning) or it can be prepared by the careful heating of sugar to produce a soluble brown colour, suitable for use in foodstuffs. It can be made at home, but it is rather tricky; if under-cooked it is weakly coloured, so that large amounts have to be added, if over-cooked it tends to be insoluble, and to impart off tastes. Some home brews tend to have an insipid-looking colour and will benefit by a small addition, added preferably before boiling the wort. I recently tried one from Leigh-Williams, which seems to meet all requirements, especially that of not altering the taste of the finished beer.

New recruits to the craft should realise that colouring beer will not make a pale ale into a stout, any more than the addition of green dye would make it creme de menthe. In fact, the whole point of a good quality caramel is that it alters only the colour, and no other property.

The method of use of the caramel I tested is extremely simple, a 50/50 blend of the caramel and water is made, and up to one-third of a pint is used in each four gallons of beer. This can be added when boiling, or later. I have found, for minor alterations of shade, a teaspoonful of the undiluted stuff added to the boiler is quite satisfactory.

It is as well to remember, that *diluted* caramel is a sugary solution and is liable to become contaminated with wild yeasts, etc, if not stored carefully. This could cause trouble if added after boiling. Trouble has been caused in commercial breweries due to lack of care in this matter.

CHAPTER VI

HOPS

Beer is almost invariably flavoured by boiling hop flowers in the wort. This imparts a bitterness and an aroma, the intensities of which vary from beer to beer.

For various reasons the amateur brewer is restricted in his choice of hops. It is not usual to be able to buy hops of a particular sort or season. It is best to buy them from your specialist supplier rather than trust to various shops who do not understand brewing, and may well have hops in stock, deteriorating all the time, for years.

The two principal varieties of hop grown in the UK are Fuggles, used for mild and brown ales, stouts and the like, and Goldings, which make the fine pales and bitters with a characteristic aroma. British hops invariably contain seeds, which are not really useful in brewing. British hops are not really suitable for the preparation of high quality lagers, but reasonable varieties can be made using the best available hops, for preference "Goldings". The hopping rates for beer varies between 2 and 4 ounces per four-gallon brew for English top fermenting beers, and two-thirds of this figure for lager types.

Imported hops are usually seedless, and are usually smaller in the flower. The varieties include Saaz, the Pilsner hop; Hallertauer from Munich, and Styrian Goldings from what is now Yugoslavia. The last-named is suitable for making fine English Bitters and is so used commercially.

Hop concentrates are produced industrially, and are sold in your specialist shop. These are convenient to use and have the great advantage of not altering on storage. It will be necessary, if these are to be used, to make a trial to see how much is needed to replace the hop content of the recipe used. Both hops and the degree of efficiency of their use vary quite a lot, but once one has made the trial these products are standard and do not vary.

The really fine bitters of commerce (yes, there are still a few good ones left!) have a pronounced hop aroma.

Now it is important, when making a quality beer, that the wort is boiled thoroughly in the presence of the hops. During this boiling, even if a cover is used, much of the essential oil of the hops is driven off and lost. Usually the whole family complains about the house smelling like a brewery. (It IS a brewery, so why not?)

To get over this loss of essential oil, which contributes most of the aroma, some home brewers keep back part of the hops until the last five minutes or so of the boiling time. This helps the aroma, but it does mean that a lot of the other ingredients remain in the hops and are wasted. Hops are, after all, our dearest raw material. Some professional breweries used to resort to the practice of "dry hopping". A small amount of fine quality hops were added to the barrel before despatch from the brewery.

Hops, however high in antiseptic principles, are not necessarily sterile, and occasionally infections were introduced, causing spoilage of the beer. In more leisurely times the casks were set up on a stillage and the beer was drawn off by a tap, so that the hops remained undisturbed while the beer was used. When various pumping devices were employed, the hops could get drawn up into the beer, spoiling its appearance and probably causing blockages. This is not relevant to the amateur, who could still use dry hopping when making draught beers.

Fortunately, the problem can be solved quite simply, even when making bottled beers. Hop oil is available to the home brewer. I have found by trials that an addition of one drop of this oil in each gallon of the beer makes a great improvement in aroma. It is expensive, so measure it accurately. The oil is best added to the beer in the second stage, after it has been in the jars three days or so.

This ensures that the oil is not wasted by being carried down with the yeast deposit, but there is still sufficient movement in the beer to disperse it. When making trials the most useful arrangement is to add the oil to half the jars of a brew, the untreated ones serving as "controls".

Beers can be made without hops, using other herbs for flavouring.

CHAPTER VII

YEAST

Yeast is one of the oldest plants domesticated by man.

For many years in baking and brewing wild yeasts were used. The housewife used to save a lump of dough over from each week's baking to start the next batch.

Even today some commercial types of breads in Germany are made in this manner. The real experienced Klondike miners were referred to as "sour doughs" because they had been there long enough to run out of bicarbonate of soda, and reverted to the old way. With the exception of the Belgian beer "Lambic", wild yeasts are no longer employed in European-type brewing practice. Fresh yeast is an unstable substance, and unless carefully preserved soon goes "off". Dried yeasts were apparently developed in Germany towards the end of the nineteenth century, and now, as everybody who reads *Winemaker & Brewer* knows, are made all over the world in a large variety of types.

Fresh bakers's yeast *can* be used for beer brewing, but is not really satisfactory. It will not settle well, and carries an "off taste". A wide range of dry and liquid yeasts is available at your specialist shop.

They are clean and stable on storage. Nevertheless, once a home brewer has acquired skill and pride in his output, he will progress to a more suitable strain. Wine yeasts are useless for beer brewing. In fact, trouble has been known to occur in breweries due to infection by *Saccharomyces ellipsoideus* strains. Those of us who make both wine and beer in small kitchens would do well to watch this point. Beer yeasts make poor wines too!

There are two main types of beer yeast, the top fermenting which is characteristic of British brewing practice, and the bottom fermenting yeasts used to prepare lagers. There is a great deal of difference in the habits of the two types, and in the properties and palate of the finished beer. Many of the yeasts sold as "beer yeast" to the amateur winemaker are of the bottom fermenting variety. They are good of their kind, and true to type. They have their advantages in that they will continue to ferment at exceedingly low temperatures, and settle down hard. They tend to be a little slower than top fermenting yeasts. If a lager is what you want, they are essential. Nevertheless, some home brewers use bottom fermenting yeasts for all types of beers. My experience is that for the best results one should stick to the appropriate variety. When ordering, be sure to specify the kind you want.

Top fermentation yeasts are quite unmistakable in action. A few hours after pitching the wort, a thick, rough, frothy mass of yeast covers the surface. This is removed by skimming, to prevent the yeast dying and dropping down into the beer, where it could cause "off" tastes. A "yeast-bitten" beer has a spectacularly foul bitter flavour, once tasted, never forgotten! Fermentation temperatures of 18-22°C (65-70°F) are appropriate for top-fermenting yeasts. Whereas most bottom-fermenting yeasts are a pure race, the general practice in British brewing does not favour this. I will not stick my neck out by extrapolating into entirely different fields! The Vinotex range has a lager yeast and two top fermenting varieties, ale and stout, all three of which I have tried and found reliable. Current practice in the Basildon area, where for various reasons there are quite a few highly productive and efficient home brewers, favours the use of cultures from commercial beers. Most commercial beers do not contain any yeast, but there are some, and those the best, which are naturally conditioned. Red Label Bass, White Label Worthington and Guiness's Extra Stout are the three most likely to be obtainable generally. Good results are obtainable from all of them. The drill is quite simple. Obtain a half-pint bottle of the beer and let it stand undisturbed for two or three days. Then pour out all but the last half inch, fill the bottle with 6oz or so of sterile wort or culture medium, fit a Handy lock by means of a rubber ring and set in a warm place for three or four days. Then use this to start your beer. The culture medium found by trial to be the most favourable is:

1 dessertspoonful malt extract
1 dessertspoonful sugar
180ml (6 fl oz) water

Boil, cool, add a good pinch each of citric acid and ammonium phosphate and one strong compound of aneurine tablet B.P.C.

When collecting yeast for future brews, it will be found that the best and cleanest yeast is obtained from the jars in the second stage of our process. This can readily be stored in the refrigerator, using a screw-stoppered jar. Remember to slacken off the lid half a turn until the yeast is chilled.

Yeast from the top of a brew, if not discoloured, can be preserved similarly. If your yeast develops a bad smell, throw it away and start a fresh culture. In an emergency the bottoms of three pint bottles of home brew will be enough to start a brew off. Of course, the more skilful you become the less yeast there is in the bottles, and it could be that you will have to call in a thirsty friend to help out. In this area one does not need to call very loudly! In any case, no self-respecting Free Brewer would refuse a charge of yeast to a colleague in distress. Even if knocked out of bed at 11.30! Any other pretext would have brought my ancestral cannon into action but fast.

Yeast nutrients, by the way, are seldom or never needed in the production of beer. A properly formulated beer wort has in it everything necessary to nourish the yeast during the fermentation.

"Consult your specialist"

CHAPTER VIII

FORMULATION

MANY home brewers go their whole lifetime using recipes from books, or from friends. This is fair enough, if the recipes suit their water and their palate. Unfortunately, many get hold of a bad recipe, produce terrible beer and give up in disgust. Others get used to it, as they did to some of the "Country wines" of a bygone era, simply because it is alcoholic and cheap. Even a good recipe, yielding a first-class brew, may not be to your palate. Look at some of our excellent commercial brews, which some folk just cannot get to liking. This is inevitable with any product having strong individual characteristics. It is one reason for the tastelessness of mass produced foods. You cannot please everybody, so knock out the flavour then you will offend nobody, except connoisseurs, who are in a minority!

Apart from these considerations, the object of home brewing is to get the beer the way you want it. No real craftsman is ever satisfied with his work, and seeks always to improve it. There is no royal road to success in home brewing. Reading helps, especially if you have enough scientific background to study professional works on brewing. Even books intended more for the general reader can often provide background knowledge, which is exceedingly helpful. Your public library will be found invaluable, and can get almost any book you need, especially if you are a serious student. It is all rather like a jigsaw puzzle, when the key piece turns up, the whole picture rapidly comes together. Clean, systematic working using measures, hydrometer and thermometer are essential. So is the keeping of records. Don't just make a change or, worse still, several changes at once, without keeping records. It would be galling to produce the beer of a lifetime, and be unable to reproduce it.

Above all else, learn as much as you possibly can about your raw materials, from all possible points of view. Find out why a particular ingredient is used in a given recipe, if necessary make a brew without it, or using more or less than the norm. Reasons which are good and sufficient in commercial breweries are not always applicable to our considerations. For example, professional brewers derive the greater part of their fermentable carbohydrates from pale malt grains. This is, for them, the cheapest and most expeditious method. As far as we are concerned it is troublesome, time consuming and expensive.

So it is that the majority of home brews are based on malt extract. Some home brewers prefer to use dried malt extracts in powder form because they find them easy to handle. I very rarely do; having served my time as a paint technologist, the handling of sticky liquids is no problem to me. Moreover, it is simpler to measure liquid malt extract into a jug than to weigh a lot of light, sticky powder. This is for the home brewer to decide.

Next, choose what sort of beer you want to make. Just for example, Stout. Stouts invariably contain patent black malt. If you wish to make a good, full bodied stout, some barley is needed. Are you going to use grains as they come, or does the increased solubility and cleanliness of flaked barley outweigh the increased cost? Is it to be slightly harsh, or do you want to round off the flavour? In which case some crystal malt is indicated. If a sweet stout is wanted, an addition of lactose would help. How bitter is it to be? Remembering that a heavy beer needs a higher hopping rate for the same apparent bitterness as for a lighter beer. Is your water supply suitable for stouts, if not, what treatment is needed to make it suitable? How strong is the beer to be? Sugar increases strength, but not flavour, unless special grades are used. Excess sugar relative to the other ingredients gives a thin beer, although the cheapness of it is a temptation to use too much.

Look out other recipes for similar types of beer, your own and other people's. See how they overcame the difficulties, or how far they fell short of what you want. There are many published recipes which show a lack of understanding of the properties of the raw materials. For example, it is pointless mashing a mixture of patent black malt and flaked barley. There is little or no diastase in the barley, and the patent black malt is heated way above the point at which its enzymes are destroyed. Unless diastase is added, either by a good diastatic malt extract, or by using pale malt grains, the barley will be unconverted, starch will be carried forward into the wort, and off tastes will be caused. Moreover, black malt yields very little fermentable carbohydrates, so if the deficit is supplied by cane sugar, a very thin beer will result.

Working out the strength of the beer is often a problem to many amateur brewers. We do not want to make a soft drink, or a heavy wine type beverage. The original gravities of commercial beers vary between 1.030 and 1.072, from mild ale to the heaviest barley wine type. This range will be found quite adequate for home brewers, below it you get almost a soft drink and only my Yuletide at 1.085 goes

40

above this figure. This admittedly is a special brew, not for everyday usage. The best way of computing an original gravity is to relate everything in terms of sugar, and read from a table of gravities. Cane sugar in its various forms is of course 100% malt extract and invert sugar 80%, while the various malts and grains can, for our purposes, be taken as about 70%, depending on the efficiency of mashing and sparging. Patent black malt, however, adds very little extract and can be omitted from the reckoning by home brewers. If it is important to work to a specified original gravity, keep back some of the sugar, and add it bit by bit until the desired figure is reached. Gravities are measured at 60°F, a correction of 0.00023 per °F. should be subtracted if below this figure, or added if above it.

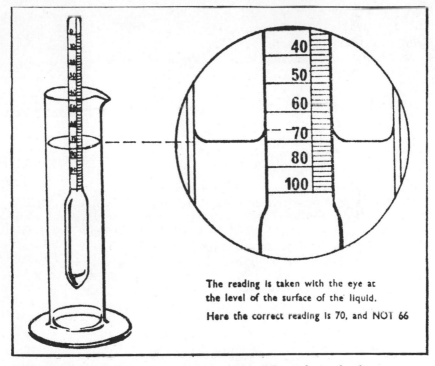

The reading is taken with the eye at the level of the surface of the liquid.

Here the correct reading is 70, and NOT 66

The specific gravity of a wort is measured by using a hydrometer, or saccharometer.

Now, after learning anything, comes the job of applying your knowledge. Here is a recipe for a stout. See if you can predict the properties of it from the recipe, then make it up for yourself.

FINN MacCOOL

(Recipe for 4 gallons nominal)

Ingredients:

450g	(1lb)	Patent black malt (coffee milled)
225g	($\frac{1}{2}$lb)	crystal malt (coffee milled)
450g	(1lb)	flaked barley
900g	(2lb)	malt extract
730g	(1lb 10oz)	sugar
85g	(3oz)	hops

6.75 litres (1$\frac{1}{2}$ gallons) water

Water treatment as appropriate

Method:

Mash at 65°C (150°F) or as close as possible for $\frac{3}{4}$ of an hour, bring to the boil. Add hops, 85g (3oz); strain on to white sugar, 730g (1lb 10oz); sparge and make up to 19.0 litres (4$\frac{1}{4}$ gallons). Cool to 27°C (80°F) max., and pitch with a real brewer's yeast. Ferment 5-7 days, rack into gallon jars.

Bottle after about a week into pint bottles, leave 2-3 weeks before use.

TECHNIQUE:

Technique is almost as important as proper formulation, in the production of good beers. After all, one must strive to get the full potential from the materials used, in order to have a really creditable beer for the time and money expended.

One's friends will not drink beer for ever if all that can be said of it is that it is alcoholic and free. It may be thought pointless to strive to make exact matches of proprietary beers but it can be done, and imitation is the sincerest form of flattery! Dave Line's excellent book "Brewing Beers Like Those You Buy" contains over 100 recipes, featuring worldwide famous beers for you to try.

For normal home brews we must accept the limitations inherent in "naturally conditioned" beers, of having just a little sediment and needing care in pouring out. Of course, for show purposes, it seems that one can chill and rebottle, but it is not really feasible for production. The same goes for filters. If you filter, you will have to carbonate as well, and you will need a brewery to put all the gear in. The cost will be so great that the *interest* on that amount of capital would buy beer for any normal drinker.

WATER TREATMENT

Most domestic water supplies in the United Kingdom are basically good brewing waters. The only problem waters are those which contain excessive amounts of chalk and this state is rarely serious. From experience the majority of people know whether water is hard or soft. If you reckon your water is hard then assume it contains chalk. Any doubt about it can easily be solved. Simply boil one gallon of water for a quarter of an hour and let it cool. Any chalk present will form a film or deposit on the boiler bottom. So now we have two categories for our water treatment: those with chalk and those without it.

Treatment for 25 litres (5 gallons) of water

Type of Beer	Chalky Water	Non-Chalky Water
Lager	1	—
Light Ale, Bitter, Pale Ale, Strong Ale, Barley Wine	1,2	2
Brown Ale, Winter Ale, Mild Ale, Sweet Stout	1,3	3
Irish Stout	—	4

1. Add 1 teaspoon of Flaked Calcium Chloride or Lactic Acid Solution; *or* boil water for a quarter of an hour and rack off the soft water for use when cool.
2. Add 1 teaspoon of Gypsum (Calcium Sulphate) and $\frac{1}{2}$ teaspoon of Epsom Salts (Magnesium Sulphate).
3. Add $\frac{1}{2}$ teaspoon of Common Salt (Sodium Chloride).
4. Add 1 teaspoon of chalk (Calcium Carbonate).

Note: One level teaspoon = 5 ml.

Finings are very useful, which are handy and economical. This is added a couple or three days before bottling, while in the gallon jars. It is not easy to make a clear draught beer without something of this nature. Beware of over-fining, and leaving too long between fining and bottling, if there is *no* yeast there will be no "condition". Stouts do not seem to need fining.

HEAD AND CONDITION

There is often confusion between the terms "Head" and "Condition".

"Condition" means the amount of carbon dioxide dissolved in the beer. If this arises as a result of fermentation in the bottle the beer is referred to as "naturally conditioned". On the other hand, if this effect is accomplished by forcing carbon dioxide into the beer by cooling and pressure, the terms "carbonated" or "artificially conditioned" are used. Naturally conditioned beer is reckoned to have a finer flavour, but the necessary yeast content and maturing time involved are commercially disadvantageous.

The "head" on a beer is caused by the carbon dioxide coming out of solution, forming bubbles which remain for a longer or shorter time on the surface of the beer. If a beer tends to lose condition too rapidly one gets a good head, for a short time, but the beer rapidly becomes flat. Some beers tend to hold tenaciously to their condition, and never really have much head, but do not get flat even if one takes an hour over the pint.

Head retention is a surface tension problem for the most part. The use of certain detergents in cleaning bottles or gear (or tankards) can destroy head retention very rapidly. The molecules migrate to the surface and quantities almost beyond the reach of the most refined analytical technique can produce this effect.

Grease is also harmful. You may sometimes notice this when eating a meal of bread and cheese with a pint. I believe that protein degradation products promote head retention. I have noticed that darker beers seem always to have better head retention.

A curious thing is that beers made with Edme Superflavex invariably have better heads than if DMS is used. Yet both of these are of uniformly good quality and never seem to vary from batch to batch. The manufacturers state, and I have no reason to think otherwise, that the analytical constants are for all practical purposes the same. This effect could easily be checked by using Superflavex to replace DMS in, say, "Double Daphne". I had to do it once when I forgot to order in time. Black malt, flaked barley and especially the new low nitrogen wheat flour additive "Brumore", also give good head retention.

Heading liquids contain something like an extract of quillaia bark. Root liquorice solutions have also this property, but since they spoil the flavour of the beer are hardly useful to a serious brewer. They also give a "false body" and are banned by law from use in commercial beers, probably for this reason. Substances of this order are also used in fire-fighting foam solutions.

Personally, I don't worry a great deal about the head on homebrew, unless the type normally has one. If one of my stouts came out headless, I would start checking back. Quite bluntly, in commercial practice a head is very profitable indeed. A given volume of CO_2 costs a lot of less than the same volume of beer! A little bit of extra gas on the keg is nearly as good as finding gas in the North Sea.

However, competition is more effective than legislation, which is why I am writing this and you are reading it.

SIMPLIFYING MEASUREMENT

If one is to produce a consistently good beer, the materials must be added in the right amounts. For experimental brewing, this is even more important. However, some materials are a nuisance to weigh, and others are required in a very small amount, water treatments for example. This is well recognised in chemical laboratories, where the volumetric principle is widely used for rapid analysis.

If compressed hops are used, they can be "weighed" quite well for our purpose with a ruler and sharp knife. For grains, just measure the volume in a graduated jug of one pound of each item and keep a note of it. A table can thus be compiled for all dry ingredients. Housewives can buy a measure directly calibrated for such things as rice, sugar, flour, etc., maybe somebody will make a Home Brewers measure. Some material, like Barbados sugar, will not fill level; here the trick is to put, say, 140g (5ozs.) of water in the jug, then add the sugar. The water makes a level to read by. Malt extract is usually sold at an SG of 1.400, which means that 450g (1lb.) occupies about 350ml (11.4fl. ozs.) Much easier than messing about counterposing jugs on kitchen scales. Unless you have served your time as a paint technologist or the like accurate and non-messy handling of treacly fluids is a problem.

Whether in our old Imperial system of measurement or metrically it is quite easy to make standard solutions of the materials we use in home brewing.

Twenty five mls made up to 500mls, or 1fl.oz. made up to 1 pint is a 5% solution, 50mls made up to 500mls (or 2fl.oz. to 1 pint) 10%, and so on.

I say "made up to one pint" not "added to", since in that case the volume would be greater than one pint.

In this way it is easy to add small percentages to brews, of such things as citric acid, bisulphite, and the like. Water treatments can be dispensed in a similar manner.

For example, a good pale ale water has from 30 to 40 parts per million of magnesium, as sulphate. Now, the crystals of Epsom salts are $MgSO_4$ $7H_2O$, which is, for our purposes, 10% of magnesium. Dissolve 60g (2oz.) of the crystals in 570ml. (1 pint) of water, and one has a solution containing 1% Mg, ie 10,000 parts per million. Since there are 4,800ml. (160fl. oz.) in 4.5 litres (1 gallon), it can be seen that 30ml. (1 fl. oz) of the stock solution will put 31 ppm in 9 litres (2 gallons) of water. Unfortunately, plaster of Paris, the commonest additive, is not very soluble. However, not to worry, in this case one just adds an excess, what is not dissolved simply settles out.

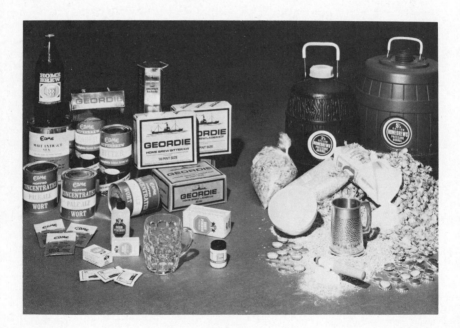

DESIGNING AND EXPERIMENTING

This chapter is respectfully dedicated to all employers of scientific and technical personnel in Great Britain, for their great, though unconscious contribution to the progress of our craft in that they drive people to drink but omit to pay them enough to afford the commercial product.

Experiments are a way of asking questions of nature. It is helpful to know what question one wants answering, and how to ask it, and it is the purpose of this chapter to show how the experimental method can be applied to Home Brewing.

The most important thing is to take accurate and full notes.

The next most important thing is not to change too many variables at once. Dabbling in this fashion is one of the reasons for some of the quite fantastic recipes and processes of the past. It is also important not to add gratuitous variables, by careless weighing and measuring. There is usually a slight variation between different batches of new materials, and the best way of overcoming this is to purchase sufficient for the series of tests in one lot. Fortunately this does not apply to sugar, which is very nearly chemically pure.

In strict form, it is as well to remember that brewing is a biological operation, and to ensure the highest accuracy tests should be duplicated at least. Fortunately we don't usually have to go to such lengths, which is as well, because even my friends could not absorb the excess gallonage resulting.

There is the old laboratory joke about duplicate tests, "It's no good doing duplicates, because you've then got to do the third run to decide which result is more probable!" For an important brew it is usually sufficient for our purposes to make it twice and get another brewer to do one. Plenty of folk seem to have books in print where the ratio of experiments to recipes appears to be 1 to 27, so perhaps I am unduly squeamish. It is possible to design an experiment to elucidate more than one point in the same series of tests.

Some of the "craft" here are at the point where if you leave the Epsom Salts out of a "Double Daphne" they can tell you what you have done, on one glass! But these are brewers as well as tasters, and that beer is our Model T, made in quantity.

For tasting beers, usually they are served in threes, two of which are alike, the idea being to spot the odd man out.

This series of tests is designed to compare "Glucose Chippings" with household sugar, and to ascertain what difference is made by using lager yeast as opposed to a top fermenting yeast. If you are a keen type there is also the possibility of making yet another pair of trials using inverted sugar made at home by boiling with citric acid.

Claims are made for Glucose Chippings and other inverted sugars by interested parties, and the only fair way of deciding whether the increased cost is worthwhile is to make an objective trial. As sold, glucose chippings are about 35p per lb, and since they contain one molecule of water it takes about 5lb to do the work of 4lb of household sugar, as will be seen from the results.

Household sugar is cheap because it is available everywhere in large quantities, and the tendency is for grocers to use it as a "loss leader" to attract custom.

The basic recipes for the beers are the same but the Wendy I and II are both ales using a top fermenting yeast and Helen I and II are both lagers using a bottom fermenting lager yeast.

WENDY

Ingredients:

900g	(2lb)	DMS (Edme)
225g	(8oz)	Brewing flour
225g	(8oz)	crystal malt, lightly cracked
		Pale ale water treatment

6.75 litres (1½ gals) water 65°C (150°F) or as close as possible
Mash for ¾ hour, add

55g	(2oz)	hops

Method:

Boil for 30 minutes, strain on to sugar, make up to 4¼ gallons, cool to 24°C (75°F), pitch with yeast, ferment six days, rack into gallon jars, rest one week and bottle into pint bottles, priming each with ½ teaspoonful white sugar.

Now here are the differences between the sisters:

"Wendy", Type I, had 900g (2lb) of glucose chippings (OG 1.040). "Wendy", Type II, had 900g (2lb) of white sugar (OG 1.044). The difference in OG being due to the water content of the glucose chippings. Red Label Bass yeast is used.

HELEN

"Helen", Type I, had 900g (2lb) of glucose chippings (OG 1.040). "Helen", Type II, had 900g (2lb) of white sugar (OG 1.045).

To each of these one level teaspoon of salt and of citric acid was added prior to fermentation. Vierka XXXX dried lager yeast used. On completion this pair of beers was served chilled.

Conclusions. Both "Wendys" were considered highly acceptable, but the majority opinion was that the Type I, made with glucose chippings, was the better of the pair, being cleaner on the palate and "drier". The fermentation appeared marginally faster.

The "Helens" also were very popular, the preference going towards the Type I, but not by so clear a margin as for the top fermented beers.

It may be due to there being more "pale" drinkers than lager users, many of whom add lime and thereby disqualify themselves from consideration as serious drinkers. It was known before the trials commenced that a better lager could be made by closed fermentation throughout, but it was desired to ascertain whether an acceptable product could be made in the manner shown.

It is interesting to note that these trials tend to prove that strength and quality are not the same because the preference went to the weaker beers.

So there it is, ladies and gentlemen of the jury. If you want the highest quality, then the glucose chippings merit your consideration, and you will have to decide for yourself on the question of costs.

When ready for bottling, sugar is added to "prime" the brew and the beer is siphoned from the fermenting vessel into the bottles

CHAPTER X

RECIPES FOR QUALITY BEERS

It is often the fashion to give many recipes in a book of this kind. Unfortunately perhaps for my bank balance, I prefer to give only those formulations which have been made up and approved by myself and my friends who follow the Craft. Everybody has his own preferences in beer, some of these brews will inevitably be more popular than others. I can, however, guarantee that, if the instructions are followed correctly a drinkable beer will be produced.

Recipes given are:
> PINK LINE LAGER – a Caribbean-style beer
> GOLDILOCKS – a light beer
> GHYLLGROVE – pale ale
> GOOD HOPE – a traditional "English bitter"
> PREMIUM GRADE BITTER
> STEPHANIE – high grade pale ale
> YULETIDE ALE – a very strong "barley wine"
> YULETIDE ALE – Mark II
> MILD MAISIE – a mild beer
> ALISON'S ALE – a brown ale
> BURTON STRONG ALE – a strong, brown ale
> OTTLEY STRONG ALE – a strong, brown ale
> INDEPENDENCE BROWN ALE – a strong, brown ale
> SIOBHAN – brown ale
> PADDY'S DELIGHT – a stout
> ILONA – a special stout
> PORTER

PINK LINE LAGER

Original gravity 1.046 at 15°C (60°F)
Recipe for 5 gallons

Invert 900g (2lb) sugar by cooking with 1 level teaspoon citric acid and 570ml (1 pint) of water until golden colour. Cool, dilute to 4.5 litres (1 gallon) and run into fermenting vessel.

Ingredients:

1.3kg	**(3lb)**	**DMS**
225g	**(8oz)**	**flaked maize**
110g	**(4oz)**	**crystal malt**
		1 level teaspoon of salt
6.75 litres (1½ gals.) water		
55g	**(2oz)**	**hops**

Method:

Mash for 45 minutes at 65°C (150°F) or as close as possible, add 55g (2oz) hops, boil for 30 minutes.

Strain off, run into fermenting vessel, and make up to 5 gallons. Cool to 24°C (75°F), add a lager yeast starter. Vinotex, Grey Owl or Vierka liquid cultures are all good.

After 36 hours fit a fermentation lock. You can either allow this to run right out for 10-14 days or rack half-way into a similar vessel. Rack, prime with 55g (2oz) sugar in 280ml (½ pint) of water, bottle and mature for three weeks.

If needed a proprietary priming/fining mixture can be added. I haven't yet tried it out, but it seems likely that by putting a pinch of dry beer finings into a high speed coffee mill with the sugar, a similar product could be prepared at home. Either way don't overdo finings at this stage.

Serve chilled to 7°C (45°F).

"GOLDILOCKS"

Now here is a new light beer which you may like to try. All my beers are named, and there are various reasons for this choice of name; it is after all a golden colour when finished and besides "Three beers are enough for a lady."

This recipe is for a 4-gallon batch and the original gravity is 1.044 at 60°F.

Ingredients:

900g	**(2lb)**	**malt extract**
225g	**(½lb)**	**crystal malt (cracked or coffee milled)**
225g	**(½lb)**	**flaked maize**
55g	**(2oz)**	**hops**
900g	**(2lb)**	**sugar**
		Pale ale water treatment
6.75 litres (1½ gals.) water		

Method:

Mash at 65°C (150°F) or as close as possible, add 55g (2oz) hops. Boil for 30 minutes, strain on to 900g (2lb) white sugar.

Sparge, make up to $4\frac{1}{4}$ gallons, cool to 27°C (80°F), pitch with a top fermentation brewer's yeast.

Ferment five to seven days, skimming as necessary, rack into gallon or 2-gallon jars with locks, allow to stand one week or until nearly clear. Fill into pint bottles and prime with half a teaspoonful white sugar to each bottle. Leave three weeks to mature.

GHYLLGROVE PALE ALE

Original gravity 1.038
Recipe for 4 gallons

This beer is prepared by using whole barley "popped" after the manner of a famous breakfast food.

The grain was heated under a grill, in a layer half an inch thick, with constant stirring. The grains nearly all popped, and very few browned.

Ingredients:

225g	**($\frac{1}{2}$lb)**	**popped barley, cracked**
900g	**(2lb)**	**malt extract**
6.75 litres (1$\frac{1}{2}$ gal.) water		
		1 level teaspoonful plaster of Paris, or water treatment as appropriate
		Mash at 65°C (150°F) or as close as possible for three-quarters of an hour raise to boil, add
55g	**(2oz)**	**hops**

Method:

Boil for 30 minutes, stand a few minutes and strain on to 900g (2lb) white sugar. Wash spent grains, make wort up to just over 4 gallons. When not over 25°C pitch with a good ale yeast.

Ferment for seven days, rack off into gallon jars, adding LW dry beer finings made up as directed, three days after racking. Leave in the jars for a total of one week, bottle in pint bottles. adding a scant half-teaspoonful of white sugar to each. Leave two weeks to condition. This beer also performs satisfactorily on draught. The colour is rather pale, a small addition of caramel to the boiling stage can be used. Heading liquid, added to the beer a day prior to racking, may be found helpful, but don't overdo it, or you can get a scene reminiscent of a lovely old Will Hay film I once saw!

GOOD HOPE

Recipe for 4 gallons

This is in the traditional "English Bitter" idiom, and was brewed by Mr James Mitchell, another of the highly skilled fraternity who are responsible for Basildon being pronounced "Boozeldon" nowadays.

Ingredients:

1.3kg	(3lb)	malt extract
335g	($\frac{3}{4}$lb)	crystal malt (cracked or coffee milled)
1.3kg	(3lb)	sugar
85g	(3oz)	hops
		Pale ale water treatment

6.75 litres (1$\frac{1}{2}$ gals.) water

Method:

Boil for half an hour, strain on to 1.3kg (3lb) white sugar. Make up to 4$\frac{1}{4}$ gallons, rinsing the hops with part of the water. Cool to 27°C (80°F) and pitch with RLB yeast.

Ferment five to seven days, skimming as necessary, rack into 1- or 2-gallon jars, leave one week, bottle into pint bottles, priming with $\frac{1}{2}$ teaspoonful white sugar to each. Mature for three weeks. Pour carefully as for the old time Bass. This is a lovely beer, impressively smooth and pleasantly bitter.

PREMIUM GRADE BITTER

Ingredients:

1.1kg	(2$\frac{1}{2}$lb)	malt extract
335g	(12oz)	flaked barley
85g	(3oz)	hops
110g	(4oz)	crystal malt (250g (8oz) if a rounder beer is wanted)
		Water treatment as appropriate (plaster of Paris 1 level teaspoon, Epsom salts short $\frac{1}{2}$ teaspoon, or proprietary article. Both kinds tried and found satisfactory)

6.75 litres (1$\frac{1}{2}$ gals.) water

Method:

Mash at 65°C (150°F) or as close as possible for $\frac{3}{4}$ hour or to starch iodine end-point, add hops 85g (3oz). Boil for 30 minutes, strain on to sugar 900g (2lb). Make up to $4\frac{1}{4}$ gallons with cold water, cool to 27°C (80°F) maximum and pitch with a true brewer's yeast (eg Red Label Bass strain). After three days fermentation add one teaspoonful of heading liquid. Rack into gallon jars after 5-7 days, leave for a week, bottle in one pint beer bottles, priming with $\frac{1}{2}$ teaspoon sugar, leave three weeks to mature. I recently got a small sample of a "Golding" type hop, and the beer was much better for it.

YULETIDE ALE

Our ancestors used to keep the feast of Yule, that is, the Midwinter Solstice, with much feasting and drinking. Most of the revelry associated with Christmas, and Hogmanay too, is of pagan origin, and really belongs to Yule. I still keep it as such, with plenty of heavy ale! It is nearly as strong as wine, and needs plenty of time in bottle to give it a real professional finish. It keeps at least a year.

Recipe for four gallons.   Original gravity 1.085.

Ingredients:

450g	(1lb)	crystal malt (cracked or coffee milled)
1.3kg	(3lb)	malt extract
110g	(4oz)	hops
		Water treatment, as for pale ale (I used one heaped teaspoon plaster of Paris, short $\frac{1}{2}$ teaspoon Epsom salts)
6.75 litres ($1\frac{1}{2}$ gallons) water		
		Boil for half an hour, strain on to
900g	(2lb)	Barbados sugar
1.3kg	(3lb)	white sugar

Method:

Sparge hops, make up to $4\frac{1}{4}$ gallons, cool to 25°C (75°F) and pitch with a real brewer's yeast. This may need as long as 10 days in the first fermentation. Rack into one- or two-gallon jars, allow to stand at least a week, then bottle, using a little sugar to each. If it is a little slow in clearing, rack again before bottling, and use suitable finings. This ale is almost the same weight as a wine, and repays amply any care taken with it. Drink it with discretion, because it is powerful stuff. Otherwise you will feel as if there are trolls dancing on your head the next morning!

YULETIDE MARK II

Ingredients:
450g	**(1lb)**	**cracked crystal malt**
1.3kg	**(3lb)**	**malt extract**
225g	**(½lb)**	**flaked barley**
		Water treatment, as for Pale Ale

6.75 litres (1½ gallons) water

Method:
Mash at 65°C (150°F) or as close as possible for ¾ hour. Bring to the boil, add:

110g	**(4oz)**	**hops**
		Boil for half an hour, strain on to
900g	**(2lb)**	**Barbados sugar**
1.3kg	**(3lb)**	**white sugar**

Sparge hops, make up to 4½ gallons, cool to 24°C (75°F) and pitch with a true top fermenting brewer's yeast (RLB strain, Grey Owl or Vinotex are all tried and good in this class of beer). Skim as necessary and ferment down to 1.010, seven days plus. As this beer is heavy it may be found helpful to give a good rousing occasionally. Rack into gallon jars under fermentation locks, leave seven or more days before bottling. Bottle in pint bottles, prime cautiously with white sugar and mature for three or four months. Do check your bottles and closures carefully, it could be a tragedy to spoil a really fine beer like this for want of a bit of effort.

ALISON'S ALE

Here is a brown ale that you might like to try out. This is not quite so weak as the commercial varieties, some of which need a pair of sticks to help them out of the bottle. It isn't all that destructive though, combining exhilaration and thirst quenching properties in reasonable measure. It's called Alison's Ale (Daphne's second name!).

Recipe for four gallons.

Ingredients:
900g	**(2lb)**	**DMS**
110g	**(4oz)**	**Patent black malt**
225g	**(8oz)**	**crystal malt (lightly cracked)**
225g	**(8oz)**	**Brumore**
6.75 litres (1½ gallons) water		
		Mild Ale water treatment

Method:

Mash at 65°C (150°F) or as close as possible for $\frac{3}{4}$ hour then add

55g	**(2oz)**	**hops**

Boil for 30 minutes, strain on to

450g	**(1lb)**	**dark sugar (eg Sainsbury's "Soft Brown")**
225g	**($\frac{1}{2}$lb)**	**granulated sugar**

Sparge hops, make up to $4\frac{1}{4}$ gallons and cool to 27°C (80°F) (max) pitch with a top fermenting ale yeast. Ferment 5-7 days, skimming as necessary, rack into gallon jars under locks, bottle after one week, adding $\frac{1}{2}$ level teaspoonful sugar to each pint bottle. Mature three weeks before using.

"STEPHANIE"

High Grade Pale Ale

Ingredients:

1.3kg	**(3lb)**	**DMS**
225g	**($\frac{1}{2}$lb)**	**flaked barley**
225g	**($\frac{1}{2}$lb)**	**crystal malt**
6.75 litres ($1\frac{1}{2}$ gallons) water		
		Water treatment for Pale Ale
85g	**(3oz)**	**hops**
900g	**(2lb)**	**sugar**

Method:

Mash at 65°C (150°F) or as close as possible for $\frac{3}{4}$ hour. Then add 85g (3oz) hops. Boil for 30 minutes. Strain on to 900g (2lb) white sugar. Sparge hops.

Make up to 19.5 litres (4 gallons 3 pints) with drinking water, cool to not more than 27°C (80°F) and pitch with a good top fermenting brewer's yeast. Ferment 5-7 days skimming as needed. Rack off into jars under fermentation locks, leave one week. If a heading liquid is used, add 48 hours before bottling. Bottle adding $\frac{1}{2}$ teaspoon white sugar per pint. Mature for three weeks before using. This beer will stand a light chilling if correctly made. This formulation could probably be made up as a lager if suitable adjustments were made.

MILD MAISIE

This is a good round mild beer, not unduly heavy, but not lacking in body. Bottled, it makes a good brown ale. The caramel is not essential, but it is the convention around here for such beers to be brown, you will doubtless make up your own mind on the subject.

Recipe for four gallons nominal.   Original gravity 1.038.

Ingredients:

225g	(½lb)	**crystal malt (cracked or coffee milled)**
225g	(½lb)	**flaked maize**
900g	(2lb)	**sugar**
675g	(1½lb)	**malt extract**
6.75 litres (1½ gallons) water		
		Water treatment as appropriate (I used one heaped teaspoonful LW mild ale crystals)
		Mash at 65°C (150°F) or as close as possible for ¾ hour, take up to boiling, add:
55g	(2oz)	**hops**
Caramel *q s* **to shade**		

Method:

Boil for 30 minutes, strain on to 900g (2lb) of granulated sugar and make up to 4¼ gallons. When at or below 27°C (80°F) pitch with a brewer's yeast. Ferment for 5-7 days, rack into gallon jars, fit locks. Leave seven days, bottle in pint bottles with ½ teaspoon sugar to each. Or fill into barrel and prime with the equivalent amount of sugar, as a syrup. It pays to use finings, especially for draught. Add to the gallon jars three days before bottling.

The bottled beer should be ready in two weeks, the draught in about three weeks.

BURTON STRONG ALE

As I always knew it, this was a dark, fairly strong, sweetish hearty beer for the cold weather. It needs a full flavour, so this recipe is based on Superflavex Malt Extract. The original gravity is 1.055, and the recipe is for a nominal 4 gallon batch.

Ingredients:

900g	(2lb)	**Superflavex**
450g	(1lb)	**crystal malt (cracked)**
110g	(4oz)	**Patent black malt (whole)**
55g	(2oz)	**hops**
1.3kg	(3lb)	**sugar**
		Water treatment as requisite
		Caramel – sufficient to colour, about one tablespoon
6.75litres (1½ gallons) water		

Method:

Boil for 30 minutes, strain on to 1.3kg (3lb) white sugar. Sparge the spent grains and make up to $4\frac{1}{4}$ gallons. Cool to 27°C (80°F) maximum. Pitch with RLB or similar yeast, ferment 5-7 days. Rack into gallon jars. Leave 5-7 days. Bottle in pint bottles with $\frac{1}{2}$ teaspoonful white sugar to each. Store three weeks before using. If this is wanted sweeter, some lactose can be used in the second stage.

OTTLEY STRONG ALE

Four gallon brew

Ingredients:

1.15kg	($2\frac{1}{2}$lb)	**DMS**
225g	(8oz)	**flaked maize**
225g	(8oz)	**crystal malt (cracked)**
110g	(4oz)	**Patent black malt (whole)**
6.75 litres ($1\frac{1}{2}$ gallons) water		
		Water treatment for pale ale
		Mash at 65°C (150°F) or as close as possible for $\frac{3}{4}$ hour, add
85g	(3oz)	**hops (Kent Goldings)**
		Boil for 30 minutes, strain on to
900g	(2lb)	**Barbados sugar**
450g	(1lb)	**white sugar**

Method:

Make up to $4\frac{1}{2}$ gallons, cool to 27°C (80°F), pitch with a top fermenting ale yeast. Ferment 6-8 days, skimming as necessary. Rack into gallon jars, allow to stand under "locks" until just off clear (approximately one week). Bottle in pint bottles, adding $\frac{1}{2}$ teaspoonful white sugar to each. Mature at least three weeks before using. This is better served chambré

Come to that, most of the heavier, matured beers are best served that way. Chilling a strong ale seems to do it no good at all though bitters can stand a bit, and lagers quite a lot. I wonder if any brewers in warmer parts of the world ever make the heavier beers, and what they come out like, and what sort of effect they have on the drinkers. Perhaps they might drop me a line.

SIOBHAN BROWN ALE

Ingredients:

675g	(1½lb)	**Superflavex malt extract**
335g	(¾lb)	**crystal malt (cracked)**
110g	(4oz)	**Patent black malt (whole)**
55g	(2oz)	**hops**
		Mild Ale water treatment to suit water

6.75 litres (1½ gallons) water

Method:

Boil 30 minutes, strain on to **900g (2lb) white sugar.**

Make up to 4½ gallons, cool to not over 27°C (80°F), and pitch with a top fermenting brewer's yeast.

Ferment 5-7 days, skimming as necessary. Rack into gallon jars under fermentation locks, leave for one week. Bottle in beer bottles, priming with ½ teaspoon white sugar per pint. Leave to mature for three weeks before using.

This beer is named after one of the lady members in Boozeldon. It might be thought that the beer is easier to drink than pronounce, but "shove-awn" is about as near as any Saxon can get to it. It is actually a de-tuned version of Burton Strong Ale, and is very nice served as a draught beer.

INDEPENDENCE STRONG ALE

Original gravity 1.058 at 15°C (60°F). Recipe for 4 gallons.

This beer was first brewed for a party at Basildon, held to commemorate the independence of Guyana on 26th May 1966.

Ingredients:

1.15kg	(2½lb)	**Superflavex malt extract**
335g	(¾lb)	**crystal malt (cracked)**
225g	(8oz)	**Brewing flour**
110g	(4oz)	**Patent black malt (whole)**
6.75 litres (1½ gallon) water		
		Water treatment for pale ale *q s* **to suit water**
		Mash at 65°C (150°F) or as close as possible for ¾ hour, add
85g	(3oz)	**hops**
		Boil for half an hour, strain on to
450g	(1lb)	**white sugar**
900g	(2lb)	**Demerara sugar**

Method:
Sparge hops, make up to 4½ gallons, cool to 27°C (80°F) (max) and pitch with a good top fermenting brewer's yeast. If a little slow, a good rousing will help. Ferment for seven days, skimming as needed. When only a thin ring of bubbles is seen, rack into gallon jars under fermentation locks and leave one week or more. Bottle in pint bottles priming with ½ teaspoonful white sugar to each. If SG is 1.010 the sugar may be omitted. Leave at least a month before using; three months is better. These heavy beers seem almost to vinify on long maturing.

PADDY'S DELIGHT

Besides Shamrock and Shillelaghs, the Irish are famous for Stout. This recipe is my interpretation of it, a good bodied black beer, perfectly enjoyable on the 17th March or the 12th July, or for that matter on any other date!

It is *not* intended as a match for that illustrious brew which is claimed to be good for you, nevertheless I am proud of it, and my "boozing chinas" have approved it. So here it is:

Recipe for 4 gallons, 1.056 original gravity

Ingredients:

225g	(½lb)	pale malt
450g	(1lb)	Patent black malt
900g	(2lb)	DMS malt extract
		1 teaspoonful salt

6.75 litres (1½ gallons) water

Edme Super Flavex and Edme DMS malt extracts are marketed by Edme Ltd, available at your specialists.

Method:
Crack the pale malt, mix all the above ingredients with warm water, then bring up to 65°C (150°F) or as close as possible and hold for ¾ hour. Add **85g (3oz) hops,** bring to the boil and hold for 30 minutes. Strain on to **1.3kg (3lb) of the darkest sugar available,** wash the spent grains and make up to just over 4 gallons.

When it has cooled to 25°C pitch with an appropriate yeast. One from bottled stout is good, the Vinotex stout yeast is also good, and the Red Label Bass strain can be used successfully. It does pay to use a real brewer's yeast whenever possible. Apart from better flavour, they tend to settle well, so that the reduction in wasted beer more than pays for the cost. Even if you buy them new each time!

Allow the beer to ferment 5-7 days, skimming as necessary, rack into 1 or 2-gallon jars, fit locks, leave seven days. Bottle into 1 pint beer bottles with $\frac{1}{2}$ teaspoonful white sugar to each. Leave a minimum of ten days, better three weeks. This has a lovely head, it is as well to put 2 pints into three 1-pint tankards.

PORTER

Original gravity 1.046 Recipe for 4 gallons. Suitable for bottled or draught.

Ingredients:

450g	(1lb)	**Patent black malt (coffee milled)**
225g	($\frac{1}{2}$lb)	**flaked barley**
85g	(3oz)	**hops**
900g	(2lb)	**malt extract**
900g	(2lb)	**sugar**
		Water treatment (e.g. Leigh Williams' mild ale crystals)

6.75 litres (1$\frac{1}{2}$ gallons) water

Method:

Mash at 65°C (150°F) or as close as possible for $\frac{3}{4}$ hour. Take up to the boil, add 85g (3oz) hops. Boil for half an hour, strain on to 900g (2lb) white sugar. Make up to $4\frac{1}{4}$ gallons, cool to 27°C (80°F) and pitch with a suitable true brewer's yeast, Red Label Bass or Guinness (if you culture your own from bottles of commercial beers) or a stout yeast such as Vinotex. Other brands may well be as good, but these I have tried out. Ferment five to seven days, rack into one or two-gallon jars with locks, allow to stand seven days, then bottle into one-pint bottles with $\frac{1}{2}$ teaspoonful white sugar to each, or into your keg with the equivalent amount of sugar syrup. Leave 3 weeks in the keg.

This should go well with pigs trotters, then one can have a "crubeen supper", a thing which one of my tasting panel is often threatening me!

ILONA (SPECIAL STOUT)

Original gravity 1.060 at 60°F.
Recipe for 4 gallons.

Ingredients:

1.3kg	**(3lb)**	**malt extract**
85g	**(3oz)**	**hops**
225g	**(8oz)**	**flaked barley**
1.3kg	**(3lb)**	**sugar**
335g	**(12oz)**	**Patent black malt**
450g	**(1lb)**	**crystal malt (cracked)**
		1 level teaspoon salt

6.75 litres (1½ gallons) water

Method:

Mash for ¾ of an hour at 65°C (150°F) or as close as possible, add 85g (3oz) hops (Kent Fuggles). Boil 30 minutes, strain on to 1.3kg (3lb) white sugar. Sparge, make up to 4 gallons 3 pints, cool to 27°C (80°F). Pitch with a stout or other top fermenting yeast, ferment 5-7 days, skimming as necessary. End point is when a thin ring of bubbles forms in the centre of the fermentation bin.

Rack into gallon jars under locks, leave one week before bottling. Bottle, adding one-half level teaspoonful per pint, leave three weeks at least to mature. Watch it, this one carries quite a punch! Or somebody will be saying, "Is this the beer that launched a thousand hangovers?"

THE PRODUCTION OF LAGER

When I started to drink beer, the choicest brew was a fairly high-gravity well-hopped bitter. It is still my favourite, though it seems to be going the way of all good things in this ultra-democratic age. Don't suppose it will be long before the bureaucrats, the politicians and monopolists between them try to inflict a "comprehensive beer" on us!

Nowadays there is a vogue for lager, despite the fancy price. Lager does not *have* to be an anaemic expensive drink, of course. That's what we're here for! I've been doing my homework and my practical tests, and have now reached the stage where serial production is possible. One thing, though. To serve lager decently, it must be chilled, which means having a refrigerator. Warm lager is doubleplus ungood! There are quite a few points of difference between lagers and ales. Most American beer is of the lager type, and due to the use of large proportions of maize and its derivatives, and the very high carbonation preferred, does not find favour with the European palate. Equally, the visiting American often complains that our beers are flat and that we serve them warm. Takes all sorts to make a world, doesn't it?

Lagers are usually made with different varieties of hops from our top fermenting ales. Having contacts, I secured a few samples of foreign hops, with very good results. However, there are a good selection of lager yeasts available in the specialist shops.

The yeast used is of a different strain. There is no difficulty in obtaining them. I have made tests of Vinotex, Grey Owl and Vierka, with excellent results in each case. It is my considered opinion that the liquid cultures are rather better than the dried, but it isn't all that great a margin. If you brew both lagers and ales, take care not to get one strain of yeast contaminated with the other, neither will be improved by it.

Fermentation of lager is carried out in closed containers. For our use, the five-gallon fermention bin with lid are admirable.

Fit a fermentation lock by drilling a half-inch hole in the lid and using a rubber ring or grommet to make an airtight fit. The first ferments are very vigorous and a lock has rather a lot of work to do.

It needs refilling at intervals.

For regular production you will need three containers. Otherwise, all the normal ale brewing equipment will serve.

One advantage of closed fermentations is that a day or so "overtime" will not result in spoilage of the beer, which can be the case when making ales in an open fermenting vessel. This can be very helpful for people who work irregularly, or sometimes feel too tired to do anything at the end of a long day. Both things trouble me at times!

While your brew is mashing and boiling, the sugar, whether one uses household, inverted or home inverted, is dissolved in water, made up to a definite volume and poured in. Then the brew is strained off and added likewise. Finally the washings and any water needed to make up the volume go in, a good shake and then wait till it cools down to pitching heat.

There is always a little empty volume, which will accommodate the froth in the first stages. Usually it is better not to put water in the lock until the ferment is well away. Even if using the liquid yeast straight from the sachet or bottle, 36 hours suffices. After a varying period of four to eight days depending on original gravity and ambient temperature, the fermentation abates, and the beer clears partially. Then rack off into your next container and leave for seven to ten days before bottling. To bottle, rack off into a container, add the priming sugar as a solution and mix well.

Then bottle and put away to mature. Lagers can take a little longer to condition at times, but not to worry, as they are the better for it.

BASILDONER GOLDBRAU

Original Gravity 1,044
5 gallon batch

Ingredients:

900g	**(2lb.)**	**sugar**
		1 level teaspoon citric acid
570ml	**(1 pint)**	**water**
		Invert by cooking to golden colour, make up to 415 Litre (1 gallon) and run into fermenting vessel
1.3kg	**(3lb.)**	**DMS**
225g	**(8oz.)**	**crystal malt**
255g	**(8oz.)**	**Brewing flour**
		1 level teaspoon salt
6.75 litres (1½ gallons) water		
		Mash at 65° (150°F) or as close as possible, for 45 minutes, add 55g 2oz. hops (Saaz,).

BBB 4

Method:

Boil for 30 minutes, strain off, wash hops, run wort into fermenting vessel, make up to five gallons, cool to 24°C (75°F,) and pitch with a lager yeast. One can add a level teaspoonful of ammonium phosphate or a yeast nutrient. Fill the lock with water when the ferment is really vigorous. Give a shake from time to time. After about five days rack into another container. In seven to ten days the beer will be ready for bottling, rack, add 55g (2oz.) of sugar made up to half a pint with water, and bottle in crown cork bottles. Leave three weeks to mature and serve chilled.

Prosit!

ASCHEIMERBRAU LAGER

5 gallon batch
Original Gravity 1,042 at 15°C (60°F.)

The name of this beer sounds fiercely Teutonic. It is, but Ascheimer means dustbin.

Ingredients:

900g	(2lb.)	sugar
		1 level teaspoon citric acid
570ml.	(1 pint)	water
		Cook gently till the colour of barley sugar, cool, dilute to 1 gallon and run into fermenting vessel.
1.4kg	(3¼lb.)	DMS
225g	(½lb.)	crystal malt (cracked or coffee milled)
		1 level teaspoon salt
40g	(1½oz.)	Hallertauer hops
6.75 litres (1½ gallons) water		

Method:

Boil for 30 minutes, strain, sparge hops, run into fermenting vessel and make up to five gallons. Pitch with a S. Carlsbergensis starter. After 36 hours fit cork and lock. Allow to ferment for ten days, rack off and add 55g (2oz.) sugar dissolved in half a pint of water. Bottle and put aside to mature for at least three weeks, in a cool place. Pour carefully to avoid disturbing the sediment, which should only be a paint coat thick. Serve chilled.

CHAPTER XI

TROUBLE SHOOTING

If a thing can happen, it probably will. The greater the inconvenience potential, the higher the probability
—The Law of Maximum Cussedness

THIS law is one of the most fundamental laws of science. In one form or another, sometimes under impolite names, it is known to practically every technologist, engineer, chemist or what have you. It reaches out into private life too.

Why is it that a shoelace carries away on the one morning of the year that one sleeps in? Somehow it is *never* overalls you are wearing when a plate of mulligatawny takes charge, is it?

One of the most frequent sources of trouble is the use of recipes which are inherently bad. Here the remedy is obvious. Either get a reliable book by an author with honesty and ability, or learn how to formulate for yourself.

Flat or Sour

One complaint that often turns up is that *some* of the bottles in a brew are flat or even sour. Now this must be due to one or more of the bottles being inefficiently sterilised, or the closure being defective. Even the professionals suffer this at times.

Tighten up on the inspection of bottles and on the effectiveness of their seals, if crown caps have been used. If you use plastic reseals, make sure that the necks of the bottles are not chipped, and that one hasn't got a grain or two of the priming sugar stuck on the rim, preventing a good seal.

Remember not to ask too much of your sterilising medium and, above all, if you use acidified bisulphite solutions for this job, discard them when finished for the day. A friend of mine lost an entire brew by saving up the solution for the next week's bottles.

Lack of proper rinsing can cause peculiar tastes in some or all of the bottles in a brew. Too much free sulphite can cause a smell of rotten eggs to develop, and a really heavy dose would kill the yeast on which the "condition" of the beer depends.

Lack of condition (gas) in a beer can be caused by allowing the beer to mature in an excessively cold place, eg the "fridge", or a ventilated larder in winter. Omission of priming sugar, or bottling too late also does this. If one does leave the beer in the second stage too long, the best remedy is to rack all the jars into your fermentation bin and add about 5% of a vigorously fermenting wort from the next brew.

Add your priming, in this case as a syrup, rouse the beer thoroughly and bottle. If you have not got a brew in hand, then take a small portion of the yeast from the bottom of the jar (say a dessertspoonful for a 4-gallon brew) and proceed as before. This trouble can easily arise if finings are used in excess.

Too Cold

Difficulties of fermentation are sometimes met with. That very bad winter some years ago brought me a crop of callers. A good rousing and a move into the warm did the trick. Make sure that the yeast is viable before one starts a brew, it is easy enough to make up a starter bottle to check it. Packets of dried yeast should be stored sensibly, in a screw-topped jar, and the date marked on them to prevent one packet being left for too long. Infected yeast can sour a brew. If it is only just going, one can add a little bicarbonate of soda to neutralise it, and sulphite at the rate of 50 ppm or so, but really it is best to scrap it and charge that one up to experience. Of course, some people's beer is so horrid it could possibly be improved by this!

Too Little Air

Top fermentation brews don't like being covered too closely for the first few days. One of my correspondents complained of a smell of "sour vomit" in his beers, which was due to covering the fermenting vessel with airtight layers of polythene and an elastic band. I use a plastic fermentation bin and its lid.

Lager, of course, is different. Continental practice favours closed fermenting vessels. Once fermentation slows up, then the beer should go under a fermentation lock. The primitive method of fermenting out in a plastic dustbin and bottling direct causes many troubles.

If one bottles too soon, one can get burst bottles occasionally, and always a thick messy yeast deposit. If one leaves it too late there is always the chance of sour beer. In any case the oxidation spoils the flavour, and no two bottles are quite alike. Some pretend to enjoy that state of affairs, but a good craftsman should have the process under control at all times.

I consistently work to fine limits + or − 1°F when mashing and + or − 001 on my OG. Of course this is to ensure that a recipe can honestly be published, but it is an ideal to aim at. That is why most of these troubles were brought to me by other people!

Bursts

Burst bottles can be prevented by inspection for damage before use, avoiding excessive yeast concentrations and by never bottling above 1006. Undue liberality with priming sugar and storage in a high temperature can cause this trouble. Look out for heatwaves, and also when fires are lit in the autumn. Needless to say, one should never overfill bottles at any time of the year. Leave $\frac{1}{2}$in to $\frac{3}{4}$in space.

Cloudiness

Cloudy beer appears to bedevil many people. If this is due to excess yeast, then the remedy is obvious. Some strains of yeast won't settle, and it is possible for a good strain to revert to a flocculent type.

The most frequent cause seems to be insufficient boiling of the wort with hops. Those barbarous recipes calling for boiling hops in water and adding this to malt extract are particularly liable to this. Carelessness in washing the spent hops and grain can also carry forward hazy-forming material. "Starch worts" are very troublesome.

Here, the remedy is care in the mashing process. Some professional brewers add Carragheen (Irish moss, a sort of seaweed) to the wort when boiling, as "copper finings". Wort throws a deposit when boiling and another when cooling, termed "hot break" and "cold break" respectively. If absolute perfection is aimed at, the wort could, when cooled down, be racked into another vessel before pitching with yeast.

SERVING YOUR BEER

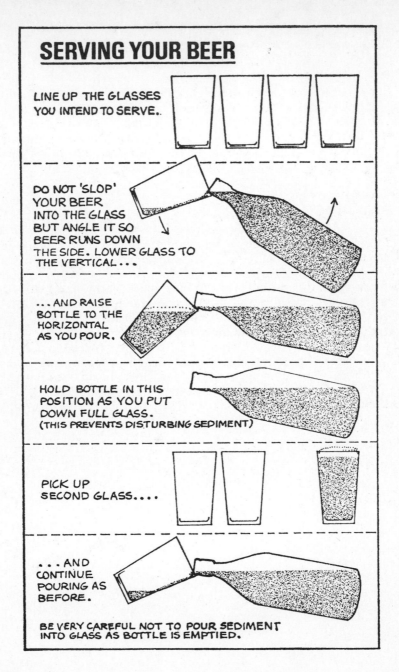

LINE UP THE GLASSES YOU INTEND TO SERVE.

DO NOT 'SLOP' YOUR BEER INTO THE GLASS BUT ANGLE IT SO BEER RUNS DOWN THE SIDE. LOWER GLASS TO THE VERTICAL ...

... AND RAISE BOTTLE TO THE HORIZONTAL AS YOU POUR.

HOLD BOTTLE IN THIS POSITION AS YOU PUT DOWN FULL GLASS. (THIS PREVENTS DISTURBING SEDIMENT)

PICK UP SECOND GLASS....

... AND CONTINUE POURING AS BEFORE.

BE VERY CAREFUL NOT TO POUR SEDIMENT INTO GLASS AS BOTTLE IS EMPTIED.

INDEX

Bold type signifies main reference

"AMATEUR WINEMAKER" BOOKS

Send large s.a.e. for our current price list

C. J. J. BERRY
HOME BREWED BEERS AND STOUTS
– the very first full-length book on this fascinating subject to be published, and still the best; many thousands of copies have been sold. Bang up-to-date, it covers: The story of ale and beer; types of beer and stout; background to brewing; brewing at home from barley, malt, malt extract, dried malt extract, other herbs and grits; how to make lager, pale ale, light, mild, brown, bitter, stout, barley wine, mock beers. Well illustrated.

DAVE LINE
BREWING BEERS LIKE THOSE YOU BUY
– over 100 original recipes to enable you to imitate famous beers from around the world. Full instructions for the beginner.

JO DEAL
MAKING CIDER
– the only book currently available on this fascinating and ultra-British craft. Recipes for sweet, dry, still and sparkling cider. And cider cookery.

BOB PRITCHARD
ALL ABOUT BEER
– the commercial brewing process described and reduced to Home Brewing terms, enabling anyone to brew really good beer with minimum effort.

DAVID MILLER
HOME BREWING FOR AMERICANS
– straightforward illustrated book, presenting a simple method of brewing using American malts, equipment and ingredients available in N. America to produce quality beers popular in America.

Edited C. J. J. BERRY
"AMATEUR WINEMAKER" RECIPES

– this useful AW paperback contains a fascinatingly varied collection of over 200 recipes garnered from several years' issues of the winemaker's favourite magazine. They include many by that well-known Birmingham winemaker Cyril Shave, a specialist in wines from herbs, and a particularly useful set of recipes for liqueurs, punches, mulls, fruit cups and other party drinks. The cartoons are by Rex Royle.

C. J. J. BERRY
WINEMAKING WITH CANNED AND DRIED FRUIT

– the simplest, most convenient and most economical of all. How to make delightful wines from the ready-prepared ingredients you can find at your grocers or supermarket, tinned fruits and juices, pulps, purées, pie fillings, concentrates, jams, jellies and dried fruit.

P. DUNCAN and B. ACTON
PROGRESSIVE WINEMAKING

– this magnificent, fact-packed volume by these two well-known winemaking experts has been hailed as one of the best books of the decade; it deals with advanced winemaking in a readable way, and carries its erudition lightly. This really fat volume – 500 pages – is really two books in one. Part I deals with the scientific theory of winemaking, sulphite, acidity, tannin, water, the hydrometer, the meaning of pH, yeast, nutrients, preparation of the must, fermentation, racking, clarification, continuous filtering, building a press, blending, fortification, wine disorders, etc. Part II deals with the production of quality wines, both red and white, and the making of Sherry, Port and Madeira type wines, and sparkling wines – all in the greatest detail. Fully illustrated.

C. J. J. BERRY
FIRST STEPS IN WINEMAKING

– the acknowledged introduction to the subject; acclaimed by thousands (over 2,000,000 have already been sold). Unbeatable at the price; winemaking clearly explained, over 150 reliable recipes, using the hydrometer; mead; cider; perry; judging; exhibiting. Illustrated.

MARION WHITTOW
GREAT FERMENTATIONS
– an honest record of one enthusiastic hobbyist's very individual approach to winemaking. Her cartoons lighten its tone agreeably.

GLADYS BLACKLOCK
MODERN WINEMAKING TECHNIQUES
– this book details the methods of juice extraction, and how to obtain the best results from a wide range of ingredients.

C. J. J. BERRY
130 NEW WINEMAKING RECIPES
– the companion paperback to *First Steps,* augmenting its 150 recipes with 130 others using newly available ingredients. Together these two books give you a unique collection of up-to-date recipes. It is also a complete instruction book in itself. Illustrations, and 50 amusing cartoons by Rex Royle.

S. W. ANDREWS
BE A WINE (and Beer) JUDGE
– an important and intensely interesting paperback by the Chairman of the Amateur Winemakers' National Guild of Judges. How to train your palate, the role of the four senses, judging techniques, making the final selection, using marking sheets, and preparing for the qualifying examination to become an accredited judge. Fully illustrated, 126 pp. Marvellous value.

DAVE LINE
BEER KITS AND BREWING
– the latest information on beer kits, hopped worts, malt extraction and new equipment. Pressure barrels and injector systems. Fully illustrated, with 50 new exciting recipes for lager, bitter, stout, barley wine, and North American beers.

PETER McCALL
DIABETIC BREWING AND WINEMAKING
– how much can a diabetic safely have – glasses of wine or pints of beer? Can he make his own wine and beer, if so what precautions should he take? Recipes for country wines and various types of low-alcohol beer that the diabetic can make.

BRYAN ACTON and PETER DUNCAN
MAKING WINES LIKE THOSE YOU BUY

– how to make your own Sherry, Port, Madeira, Champagne, Chianti, red and white table and dessert wines, hocks, Moselles, etc. A fascinating chapter tells how to make a whole range of aperitifs (Vermouth, etc) and liqueurs, and all this at a fraction of what they would cost to buy. The book for the really progressive winemaker. Seventy-six recipes for wines, 56 for liqueurs. Fully illustrated.

BRYAN ACTON and PETER DUNCAN
MAKING MEAD

– the up-to-date approach to man's most ancient drink. How to make meads (sweet and dry), melomels, hyppocras, metheglin, pyments, cyser, etc, etc. The only full-length paperback on this winemaking speciality available.

ANNE PARRACK
COMMONSENSE WINEMAKING

– a practical no frills primer in winemaking and with its aid anyone can quickly and easily be making superb wines.

ROY EKINS
WORLDWIDE WINEMAKING RECIPES

– an intriguing book of recipes ranging from prickly pears to paw paws to lychees and logans.

BRYAN ACTON
RECIPES FOR PRIZEWINNING WINES

– recipes for making your own wines are not difficult to come by nowadays: recipes which will produce *quality* wines are. That is where this book can help you. Most of the recipes that it contains have won prizes in national and regional shows, and they have been garnered over several years by Bryan Acton; others have been devised by him to guarantee first-class results. All the recipes in this book, carefully followed, will produce wines of startling quality with the minimum of effort and the maximum of certainty. So if you wish to get among the prizewinners – or even just to produce superb wines for your own satisfaction – this is the book for you!

JOE DEAL
MAKING CIDER — 2nd EDITION
Have your ever been faced with a glut of autumn apples and don't know what to do with them? In this new edition of her popular book, Jo Deal shows you how, with the minimum of equipment, you can turn them into delicious cider — sweet or dry, sparkling or still. As readers of the previous edition will testify, MAKING CIDER is a readable introduction to the subject, full of sound practical advice, and written by an acknowledged expert on domestic cidermaking. For good measure the book includes over 30 recipes to show you how to brighten up your cooking using cider!

T. EDWIN BELT
BETTER WINES FROM CONCENTRATES
It's just as easy to make a whole range of splendid wines from your favourite grape juice concentrate as the one described on the can, and this book explains how to do just that. It is an eminently practical book that avoids the temptation to blind the reader with science, and it has been clearly written by an author with more than 25 years' experience in winemaking.

C. J. J. BERRY
HINTS ON HOME BREWING
— concise and well-illustrated "rapid course" for home brewers, containing all the basic, down-to-earth essentials.

C. J. DART and D. A. SMITH
WOODWORK FOR WINEMAKERS
— have you ever wanted to make your own wine press? Or fruit pulper? Or winery? If you have, then this is the book for you. It explains how over 30 useful pieces of winemaking equipment can be made easily and cheaply at home using only the most elementary tools. The authors give clear and detailed working drawings and instructions in every case.

WILF NEWSOM
THE HAPPY BREWER
— this book caters for the home brewer who wishes to go more deeply into the theory of brewing and really understands the techniques he employs.

80